# Poems of
# John Keats

# Poems of
# John Keats

*Selected and with an Introduction
by* CLAIRE TOMALIN

PENGUIN CLASSICS
*an imprint of*
PENGUIN BOOKS

PENGUIN CLASSICS

Published by the Penguin Group
Penguin Books Ltd, 80 Strand, London WC2R ORL, England
Penguin Group (USA) Inc., 375 Hudson Street, New York, New York 10014, USA
Penguin Group (Canada), 90 Eglinton Avenue East, Suite 700, Toronto, Ontario,
Canada M4P 2Y3 (a division of Pearson Penguin Canada Inc.)
Penguin Ireland, 25 St Stephen's Green, Dublin 2, Ireland (a division of Penguin Books Ltd)
Penguin Group (Australia), 250 Camberwell Road, Camberwell, Victoria 3124, Australia
(a division of Pearson Australia Group Pty Ltd)
Penguin Books India Pvt Ltd, 11 Community Centre,
Panchsheel Park, New Delhi – 110 017, India
Penguin Group (NZ), 67 Apollo Drive, Rosedale, North Shore 0632, New Zealand
(a division of Pearson New Zealand Ltd)
Penguin Books (South Africa) (Pty) Ltd, 24 Sturdee Avenue,
Rosebank, Johannesburg 2196, South Africa

Penguin Books Ltd, Registered Offices: 80 Strand, London WC2R ORL, England

www.penguin.com

This selection first published 2009

3

Set in 10/12.5pt PostScript Adobe Sabon
Typeset by Rowland Phototypesetting Ltd, Bury St Edmunds, Suffolk
Printed in England by Clays Ltd, St Ives plc

A CIP catalogue record for this book is available from the British Library

ISBN: 978-1-846-14143-0

www.greenpenguin.co.uk

# Contents

## Odes

## A Song

## Narrative Poems

## The Natural World

## Light-hearted and Nonsense Poems

## Letters

# Introduction

John Keats took his place among the great English poets in the narrow space of six years. He was twenty when he first had a poem published in 1816, twenty-one when a first volume of his poetry appeared, twenty-two when the second followed. In the same year his work was ferociously attacked in the press, and his young brother Tom died of tuberculosis; and at the same time he fell in love with Fanny Brawne, with no prospect of marriage. His health was never good. Yet an *annus mirabilis* followed, in the course of which he wrote a series of master works that included 'The Eve of St Agnes', 'La Belle Dame sans Merci', *Lamia*, the long fragment of *Hyperion* and the great odes. All were published in July 1820, in his third and last volume. By now he knew himself to be dying. In September he set off for Italy, with no real hope that the warm climate would save him. In Rome he wrote no more. He died on 23 February 1821, at the age of twenty-five, asking that his tomb should be marked with the bitter words 'Here lies one whose name was writ in water.'

The works he left were of irresistible strength and beauty, and slowly they made their way to readers. A first collected edition appeared in 1829. Four years later Richard Monckton Milnes, a young politician with literary tastes, friend of Tennyson and Thackeray, sought out two of Keats's friends while travelling in Italy: Joseph Severn, who had made the journey to Rome with him and nursed him there, and Charles Brown, who had shared a house in Hampstead with him and preserved many of his papers. They were generous with their help, and Milnes was encouraged to collect more material. He prepared a two-volume *Life, Letters, and Literary Remains*, including more poems, eventually published in 1848. Keats's reputation grew and established itself. Tennyson declared him the greatest poet of the century, and successive generations have discovered his work with fresh wonder and steady admiration. His own words in a letter to his brother, 'I think I shall be among the English Poets after my death', have been fully borne out.

He was born on 31 October 1795, the eldest child of twenty-year-old Frances Jennings, daughter of a moneyed family owning property in the City, and her twenty-one-year-old husband Thomas Keats, a lad from the country who looked after the horses at the Swan and Hoop in Moorgate, an inn owned by his wife's father. It is not known whether John Keats was born at the Swan and Hoop, but he was a London boy, taken to St Botolph's in Bishopsgate on 18 December to be christened. Two younger brothers, George and Tom, and a sister, Fanny, followed. When John was eight his father was found dead on the road, thrown from a horse. Within two months his mother left the children to marry again and Mrs Jennings, his maternal grandmother, took charge. She sent him to an excellent boarding school in Enfield, run by the cultivated, liberal Dissenter John Clarke, whose son Charles Cowden Clarke, eight years older than Keats, became a protective friend. Another schoolfriend, William Haslam, remained devoted to him throughout his life, giving him moral and financial help to the end. The school's library encouraged wide reading, and Keats immersed himself in the English poets, Spenser a favourite. He also translated from the Latin, making a start on Virgil's *Aeneid*. He saw little of his mother, whom he loved passionately, but when he found her ill during a school holiday he was able to nurse her. The illness was almost certainly tuberculosis, and early in 1810 she died. Keats felt a strong bond of tenderness with his younger brothers and sister, as orphans who must depend on one another. There was some money due to them from their grandfather, partly tied up in Chancery, and their appointed guardians were not overly sympathetic or helpful.

A few months after his mother's death Keats left school to start on medical studies, by his own choice. The wish to help and serve the sick was important to him: at the end of his life he wrote of the necessity of being among 'those to whom the miseries of the world/ Are misery, and will not let them rest'.* He was first apprenticed to a surgeon in Edmonton and after four years entered as a student at Guy's Hospital, where he passed a qualifying examination in the summer of 1816, needing only another year in the wards to complete his professional qualifications. At the same time he was writing poetry and had a sonnet published in Leigh Hunt's radical paper, the *Examiner*. Encouraged by this, he decided to abandon medicine and give himself entirely to poetry, a bold decision in this troubled post-war period. But he did not forget, or regret, his medical studies, and in 1819 even considered returning to them.

Keats enjoyed the life of a young Londoner. His

* *The Fall of Hyperion*, Book I, line 147.

student's scribble on a friend's chemistry notebook, 'Give me women, wine, and snuff/Until I cry out "hold, enough!"', tells us he was neither an ascetic nor a recluse. He loved his friends, and his high spirits, warmth and intelligence brought him many, rich and poor, some with literary ambitions of their own, lawyers, artists and publishers. John Hamilton Reynolds was a would-be poet who settled for the law, Benjamin Bailey a wealthy undergraduate preparing to become a clergyman at Oxford; the cheerful Charles Brown had private money, travelled with Keats and shared a house in Hampstead with him, close to the family of Charles Dilke, who offered him almost a second home. The painter Benjamin Haydon entertained him in his studio, and Keats allowed him to make a life mask of his face, and lent him money he could ill afford. Another struggling artist, Joseph Severn, joined the circle; as did the good Richard Woodhouse, legal and literary adviser to the publishing firm of Taylor & Hessey. Like Haslam, they all expected great things from Keats as a writer.

With established literary figures Keats was stiffer. He knew both Shelley and Wordsworth, but was unwilling to be patronized by Shelley, and dismayed by Wordsworth's self-importance and political shift to the right. His feelings about Leigh Hunt changed from gratitude for his initial encouragement to disillusion with his frivolity, but he was again grateful when Hunt took him in during his illness in 1820.

Keats's first collection, published by Charles Ollier early in 1817, was made up of sonnets, verse letters to friends and short occasional poems. It was little noticed, except that he was immediately approached by other publishers, Taylor & Hessey, eager to publish further work of his. He started at once on a large undertaking,

*Endymion*, 4,000 lines of fanciful narrative loosely drawn from Greek myths, which he worked on for a year and saw published in April 1818. After this he took a tale from Boccaccio for 'Isabella; or, The Pot of Basil', and began *Hyperion*, planned as an epic, again drawn from Greek mythology. There is scattered brilliance in all these works and a steady growth of control, but *Hyperion* remained a fragment. Meanwhile he was reading, Shakespeare, Milton, Chaucer, Dryden, Chatterton, and his contemporaries Coleridge, Wordsworth and Byron; and listening to Hazlitt's lectures on literature.

His brothers and sister were always in his heart. He sent Fanny comic poems written to amuse her, and when George settled in America in 1818 long letters went off regularly to him and his wife. His letters were treasured by friends and family alike, and often included newly written poems. The voice is direct and vivid, quick and humorous, becoming thoughtful and intense in feeling as he explores ideas. Few poets have offered so many insights into the workings of the imagination and the process of composition. He lets us see the world he inhabits, where he is and what he is looking at, whether it is a sparrow picking about in the gravel outside his window, a river 'streaming silverly through the trees', or a lady's room, 'a very tasty sort of place with Books, Pictures a bronze statue of Buonaparte, Music, aeolian Harp; a Parrot a Linnet – A Case of choice Liquers &c &c'. Bred in London, Keats was always eager to get out into the country, and in the few years of his adult life he visited the Isle of Wight, Margate on the east coast, Oxford and Stratford-on-Avon, Devonshire, the Lake District, Scotland with a brief foray into northern Ireland, and Hampshire. Letters and poems alike draw on these travels.

But in the autumn of 1818 his eighteen-year-old brother Tom was struck down with advanced tuberculosis. Keats cared for him single-handed at his house in Hampstead, where Tom died in December. The distress and difficulty of the task wore down his own strength. During that autumn Mrs Brawne, a widow with three children, arrived in Hampstead. Keats began a flirtation with her eighteen-year-old daughter, Fanny, and was soon seriously in love. So the year ended divided between grief and excitement.

Out of these feelings came Keats's greatest work, written in 1819. In January he went to Chichester and wrote 'The Eve of St Agnes'. The spring, with many sunlit days and clear nights, was spent in Hampstead, with Fanny Brawne close by, and here he wrote the ballad 'La Belle Dame sans Merci', as well as the supremely beautiful and subtly wrought 'Ode to a Nightingale' and its companion odes, 'On a Grecian Urn', 'On Melancholy' and 'To Psyche', meditations on the fragility of human pleasures and the evanescence of all experience. In July he went back to the Isle of Wight and began work on *Lamia*, another tale set in ancient Greece, containing some of his most gorgeous and powerful writing. The witch Lamia changes herself from a snake into a woman for love of Lycius and they become lovers, but at their marriage feast his old tutor, the philosopher Apollonius, sees her true nature and by calling her name destroys her. Lycius dies horror-struck.

In August he and Brown found lodgings in Winchester, 'the pleasantest Town I ever was in', with its cathedral, water meadows, mellow houses and walled gardens. Keats took up *Hyperion* again and completed *Lamia*. The fine autumn was like a blessing on his writing. Brown departed, Keats worked on happily alone. He walked in the fields, and from this came his greatest ode, 'To Autumn'. It tells us what he saw of the season, and what he knew, setting his pleasure in the rich texture of shapes and colours, the sounds of living creatures, the swellings, pressings, oozings, bendings and plumpings, the fume of poppies and the still-budding flowers, against the 'soft-dying day', the wailing of gnats, the gathering swallows, the full-grown lambs (ready for market) and the wind, which, like everything else, 'lives or dies'. Rooted in a directly observed world, 'To Autumn' surpasses even the earlier odes with their exquisite dreams: it is a flawless piece.

This was the last contentment he knew. The swallows left, Keats returned to Hampstead, winter arrived. Although he and Fanny Brawne became formally en-gaged, he was tormented by physical longing to possess her – not allowed outside marriage with a girl of her class – and by intense, unfounded jealousy. When he showed clear symptoms of the tuberculosis that had killed his brother, the torment grew worse, since it meant there was no hope ever of consummating his love for her. In February 1820 he recognized that his illness was fatal. In May, Brown left to travel, a sad loss for Keats. He was nursed first by the Hunts and then by Mrs Brawne and a tender and loving Fanny.

He was able to oversee the printing of the volume of poems published by Taylor in July 1820 but in September, on doctor's advice, he left for Italy. Brown did not offer to go, and Haslam was unable to leave his pregnant wife, but Joseph Severn heroically went with Keats. The voyage was frightful, in a confined cabin shared with other voyagers, storms delaying them and quarantine regulations keeping them aboard for another ten days after they reached Naples on 21 October. They arrived in Rome in mid-November and moved into lodgings on the Spanish Steps. Taylor had been in touch with an English doctor in Rome, James Clark, who, having seen Keats, remarked, 'he's too noble an animal to be allowed to sink', but failed to diagnose his condition – in fact he had very little of his lungs left. Keats's plan was to kill himself with the laudanum he had brought with him. Severn got rid of the laudanum, and Keats had to comfort himself with the thought that he would soon have daisies growing over him. His last letter, to Brown, said he felt he was 'leading a posthumous existence'. He would not read Fanny Brawne's letters, but asked to have them buried with him, and kept in his hand for hours at a time the smooth white cornelian stone she had given him.

Severn's letters tell the rest. There was a brief time of respite in which Keats managed to drag himself up to the Pincio Gardens, worked at his Italian and began to think of writing a poem. But in mid-December came haemorrhages, night fevers, delusions, desperation. An English nurse was found to help through the horrors, until, in the afternoon of 23 February, Keats asked Severn to lift him, 'for I am dying – I shall die easy – don't be frightened – thank God it has come.' Severn held him until eleven that night, when at last Keats died, peacefully.

He was buried three days later in the cemetery for non-Catholics in Rome. Fanny Brawne wrote to Fanny Keats, 'I have not got over it and never shall.' Shelley mourned him by writing *Adonais*, and was drowned in 1822 with a copy of Keats's volume of 1820 in his pocket. The house in which Keats died is now the Keats–Shelley Museum.

# A Ballad

## La Belle Dame sans Merci
### A Ballad

#### I

O, what can ail thee, knight-at-arms,
  Alone and palely loitering?
The sedge has wither'd from the lake,
  And no birds sing.

#### II

O, what can ail thee, knight-at-arms,
  So haggard and so woe-begone?
The squirrel's granary is full,
  And the harvest's done.

#### III

I see a lilly on thy brow,
  With anguish moist and fever dew;
And on thy cheeks a fading rose
  Fast withereth too.

#### IV

I met a lady in the meads,
  Full beautiful – a faery's child,
Her hair was long, her foot was light,
  And her eyes were wild.

#### V

I made a garland for her head,
  And bracelets too, and fragrant zone;
She look'd at me as she did love,
  And made sweet moan.

## VI

I set her on my pacing steed,
    And nothing else saw all day long;
For sidelong would she bend, and sing
    A faery's song.

## VII

She found me roots of relish sweet,
    And honey wild, and manna dew,
And sure in language strange she said –
    'I love thee true'.

## VIII

She took me to her elfin grot,
    And there she wept and sigh'd full sore,
And there I shut her wild wild eyes
    With kisses four.

## IX

And there she lulled me asleep
    And there I dream'd – Ah! woe betide!
The latest dream I ever dream'd
    On the cold hill side.

## X

I saw pale kings and princes too,
    Pale warriors, death-pale were they all;
They cried – 'La Belle Dame sans Merci
    Hath thee in thrall!'

### XI

I saw their starved lips in the gloam,
   With horrid warning gaped wide,
And I awoke and found me here,
   On the cold hill's side.

### XII

And this is why I sojourn here
   Alone and palely loitering,
Though the sedge has wither'd from the lake,
   And no birds sing.

# Sonnets

To one who has been long in city pent,
'Tis very sweet to look into the fair
And open face of heaven, – to breathe a prayer
Full in the smile of the blue firmament.
Who is more happy, when, with heart's content,
Fatigued he sinks into some pleasant lair
Of wavy grass, and reads a debonair
And gentle tale of love and languishment?
Returning home at evening, with an ear
Catching the notes of Philomel, – an eye
Watching the sailing cloudlet's bright career,
He mourns that day so soon has glided by:
E'en like the passage of an angel's tear
That falls through the clear ether silently.

June 1816. According to Keats's brother George, 'written in the fields' on a day when he and his fellow medical students went out of London to bathe in a river and enjoy the sunshine. The first line is an echo of Milton's *Paradise Lost*, Book I: 'As one who long in populous city pent ...' All of Keats's early sonnets are written in the Petrarchan sonnet form, with the octet a-b-b-a, a-b-b-a.

# *On first looking into Chapman's Homer*

Much have I travell'd in the realms of gold,
   And many goodly states and kingdoms seen;
   Round many western islands have I been
Which bards in fealty to Apollo hold.
Oft of one wide expanse had I been told
   That deep-brow'd Homer ruled as his demesne;
   Yet did I never breathe its pure serene
Till I heard Chapman speak out loud and bold:
Then felt I like some watcher of the skies
   When a new planet swims into his ken;
Or like stout Cortez when with eagle eyes
   He star'd at the Pacific – and all his men
Look'd at each other with a wild surmise –
   Silent, upon a peak in Darien.

Oct. 1816 (first printed in the *Examiner*, 1 Dec. 1816, and revised for the
volume of *Poems* published 1 Mar. 1817).
   As close to perfection as a sonnet can be, rising in the sestet to the marvel-
lous surprise of the ending – a work of genius by a twenty-one-year-old.

# To my Brothers

Small, busy flames play through the fresh laid coals,
    And their faint cracklings o'er our silence creep
    Like whispers of the household gods that keep
A gentle empire o'er fraternal souls.
And while, for rhymes, I search around the poles,
    Your eyes are fix'd, as in poetic sleep,
    Upon the lore so voluble and deep,
That aye at fall of night our care condoles.
This is your birth-day Tom, and I rejoice
    That thus it passes smoothly, quietly.
Many such eves of gently whisp'ring noise
    May we together pass, and calmly try
What are this world's true joys, – ere the great voice,
    From its fair face, shall bid our spirits fly.

18 Nov. 1816. A fireside evening of 'gently whisp'ring noise' with George and Tom, and an awareness of how quickly such pleasures pass.

Great spirits now on earth are sojourning;
    He of the cloud, the cataract, the lake,
    Who on Helvellyn's summit, wide awake,
Catches his freshness from Archangel's wing:
He of the rose, the violet, the spring,
    The social smile, the chain for Freedom's sake:
    And lo! – whose stedfastness would never take
A meaner sound than Raphael's whispering.
And other spirits there are standing apart
    Upon the forehead of the age to come;
These, these will give the world another heart,
    And other pulses. Hear ye not the hum
Of mighty workings? –
    Listen awhile ye nations, and be dumb.

20 Nov. 1816. The great spirits are Wordsworth and Leigh Hunt, with others preparing to join them, ready to 'give the world another heart'.

# On the Grasshopper and Cricket

The poetry of earth is never dead:
  When all the birds are faint with the hot sun,
  And hide in cooling trees, a voice will run
From hedge to hedge about the new-mown mead;
That is the Grasshopper's – he takes the lead
  In summer luxury, – he has never done
  With his delights; for when tired out with fun
He rests at ease beneath some pleasant weed.
The poetry of earth is ceasing never:
  On a lone winter evening, when the frost
    Has wrought a silence, from the stove there
                       shrills
The Cricket's song, in warmth increasing ever,
  And seems to one in drowsiness half lost,
    The Grasshopper's among some grassy hills.

30 Dec. 1816. A competition sonnet, supposedly written in fifteen minutes when Leigh Hunt proposed the subject. Here is Hunt's sonnet:

> Green little vaulter in the sunny grass,
> Catching your heart up in the feel of June,
> Sole voice that's heard amidst the lazy noon,
> When even bees lag at the summoning brass;
> And you, warm little housekeeper, who class
> With those who think the candles come too soon,
> Loving the fire, and with your tricksome tune
> Nick the glad silent moments as they pass;
> Oh sweet and tiny cousins, that belong
> One to the fields, the other to the hearth,
> Both have your sunshine, both, though small, are strong
> At your clear hearts; and both were sent on earth
> To sing in thoughtful ears this natural song:
> Indoors and out, summer and winter, – Mirth.

## *To G. A. W.*

Nymph of the downward smile and sidelong glance,
    In what diviner moments of the day
    Art thou most lovely? – when gone far astray
Into the labyrinths of sweet utterance,
Or when serenely wand'ring in a trance
    Of sober thought? – or when starting away
    With careless robe to meet the morning ray
Thou spar'st the flowers in thy mazy dance?
Haply 'tis when thy ruby lips part sweetly,
    And so remain, because thou listenest:
But thou to please wert nurtured so completely
    That I can never tell what mood is best.
I shall as soon pronounce which Grace more neatly
    Trips it before Apollo than the rest.

Dec. 1816. The warmest tribute ever offered to a sister-in-law – Georgiana
Augusta Wylie was eighteen when Keats paid her this compliment. She
married George Keats eighteen months later, on 28 May 1818, just before
they emigrated to America.

After dark vapours have oppress'd our plains
    For a long dreary season, comes a day
    Born of the gentle South, and clears away
From the sick heavens all unseemly stains.
The anxious month, relieved of its pains,
    Takes as a long-lost right the feel of May;
    The eyelids with the passing coolness play
Like rose leaves with the drip of Summer rains.
The calmest thoughts come round us; as of leaves
    Budding – fruit ripening in stillness – Autumn suns
Smiling at eve upon the quiet sheaves –
Sweet Sappho's cheek – a smiling infant's breath –
    The gradual sand that through an hour-glass runs –
A woodland rivulet – a Poet's death.

31 Jan. 1817. This early sonnet remained unpublished during Keats's life-time.

When I have fears that I may cease to be
   Before my pen has glean'd my teeming brain,
Before high-piled books, in charactery,
   Hold like rich garners the full ripen'd grain;
When I behold, upon the night's starr'd face,
   Huge cloudy symbols of a high romance,
And think that I may never live to trace
   Their shadows, with the magic hand of chance;
And when I feel, fair creature of an hour,
   That I shall never look upon thee more,
Never have relish in the faery power
   Of unreflecting love; – then on the shore
Of the wide world I stand alone, and think
Till love and fame to nothingness do sink.

From a letter to J. H. Reynolds, 31 Jan. 1818.
  Not published during Keats's lifetime. He has taken up the Shakespearean sonnet form (a-b-a-b, c-d-c-d, e-f-e-f, g-g) and writes with Shakespearean boldness of metaphor.

Bright star, would I were stedfast as thou art –
   Not in lone splendour hung aloft the night
And watching, with eternal lids apart,
   Like nature's patient, sleepless Eremite,
The moving waters at their priestlike task
   Of pure ablution round earth's human shores,
Or gazing on the new soft-fallen mask
   Of snow upon the mountains and the moors –
No – yet still stedfast, still unchangeable,
   Pillow'd upon my fair love's ripening breast,
To feel for ever its soft fall and swell,
   Awake for ever in a sweet unrest,
Still, still to hear her tender-taken breath,
And so live ever – or else swoon to death.

Feb. 1819. This was thought to have been his last sonnet, but was almost
certainly written earlier. It was written on a blank page in Shakespeare's
*Poems*, facing 'A Lover's Complaint'.

Why did I laugh to-night? No voice will tell:
  No God, no Demon of severe response,
Deigns to reply from Heaven or from Hell.
  Then to my human heart I turn at once.
Heart! Thou and I are here sad and alone;
  I say, why did I laugh! O mortal pain!
O Darkness! Darkness! ever must I moan,
  To question Heaven and Hell and Heart in vain.
Why did I laugh? I know this Being's lease,
  My fancy to its utmost blisses spreads;
Yet would I on this very midnight cease,
  And the world's gaudy ensigns see in shreds;
Verse, Fame, and Beauty are intense indeed,
But Death intenser – Death is Life's high meed.

Keats proclaims his human self-sufficiency in this sonnet, sent in a letter to his brother and sister-in-law dated 19 Mar. 1819. He followed it with the words 'I went to bed, and enjoyed an uninterrupted sleep – Sane I went to bed and sane I arose' – and broke off the letter. 'Yet would I on this very midnight cease' looks forward to 'To cease upon the midnight with no pain' in 'Ode to a Nightingale', written two months later.

## A Dream, after reading Dante's Episode of Paolo and Francesca

As Hermes once took to his feathers light,
　　When lulled Argus, baffled, swoon'd and slept,
So on a Delphic reed, my idle spright
　　So play'd, so charm'd, so conquer'd, so bereft
The dragon-world of all its hundred eyes;
　　And, seeing it asleep, so fled away –
Not to pure Ida with its snow-cold skies,
　　Nor unto Tempe where Jove griev'd a day;
But to that second circle of sad hell,
　　Where 'mid the gust, the whirlwind, and the flaw
Of rain and hail-stones, lovers need not tell
　　Their sorrows. Pale were the sweet lips I saw,
Pale were the lips I kiss'd, and fair the form
I floated with, about that melancholy storm.

First printed in the *Indicator*, June 1820.

Keats described his dream, inspired by reading Dante, in a continuation of the long letter to George and Georgiana, this section dated 16 Apr. 1819: 'The dream was one of the most delightful enjoyments I ever had in my life – I floated about the whirling atmosphere as it is described with a beautiful figure to whose lips mine were joined as it seemed for an age – and in the midst of all this cold and darkness I was warm . . . o that I could dream it every night –'

## To Sleep

O soft embalmer of the still midnight,
   Shutting, with careful fingers and benign,
Our gloom-pleas'd eyes, embower'd from the light,
   Enshaded in forgetfulness divine:
O soothest Sleep! if so it please thee, close
   In midst of this thine hymn my willing eyes,
Or wait the amen, ere thy poppy throws
   Around my bed its lulling charities.
Then save me, or the passed day will shine
Upon my pillow, breeding many woes, –
   Save me from curious Conscience, that still lords
Its strength for darkness, burrowing like a mole;
   Turn the key deftly in the oiled wards,
And seal the hushed Casket of my Soul.

Another sonnet from the long letter to George and Georgiana, this section
dated 30 Apr. 1819.

# On Fame

Fame, like a wayward Girl, will still be coy
  To those who woo her with too slavish knees,
But makes surrender to some thoughtless Boy,
  And dotes the more upon a heart at ease;
She is a Gipsey, will not speak to those
  Who have not learnt to be content without her;
A Jilt, whose ear was never whisper'd close,
  Who thinks they scandal her who talk about her;
A very Gipsey is she, Nilus-born,
  Sister-in-law to jealous Potiphar;
Ye love-sick Bards, repay her scorn for scorn,
  Ye Artists lovelorn, madmen that ye are!
Make your best bow to her and bid adieu,
Then, if she likes it, she will follow you.

Yet another sonnet from the long letter to George and Georgiana, this
section dated 30 Apr. 1819 – Keats suggests these were 'dashed off' in a
hurry.

The day is gone, and all its sweets are gone!
   Sweet voice, sweet lips, soft hand, and softer breast,
Warm breath, light whisper, tender semi-tone,
   Bright eyes, accomplish'd shape, and lang'rous waist!
Faded the flower and all its budded charms,
   Faded the sight of beauty from my eyes,
Faded the shape of beauty from my arms,
   Faded the voice, warmth, whiteness, paradise –
Vanish'd unseasonably at shut of eve,
   When the dusk holiday – or holinight
Of fragrant-curtain'd love begins to weave
   The woof of darkness thick, for hid delight;
But, as I've read love's missal through to-day,
He'll let me sleep, seeing I fast and pray.

10 Oct. 1819. Written after spending a happy day with Fanny Brawne in Hampstead.

I cry your mercy – pity – love! – aye, love!
   Merciful love that tantalizes not,
One-thoughted, never-wandering, guileless love,
   Unmask'd, and being seen – without a blot!
O! let me have thee whole, – all – all – be mine!
   That shape, that fairness, that sweet minor zest
Of love, your kiss, – those hands, those eyes divine,
   That warm, white, lucent, million-pleasured breast, –
Yourself – your soul – in pity give me all,
   Withhold no atom's atom or I die,
Or living on perhaps, your wretched thrall,
   Forget, in the mist of idle misery,
Life's purposes, – the palate of my mind
Losing its gust, and my ambition blind!

Nov. 1819.

# Odes

## Ode on Indolence
*'They toil not, neither do they spin.'*

### I

One morn before me were three figures seen,
 With bowed necks, and joined hands, side-faced;
And one behind the other stepp'd serene,
 In placid sandals, and in white robes graced;
They pass'd, like figures on a marble urn,
 When shifted round to see the other side;
  They came again; as when the urn once more
Is shifted round, the first seen shades return;
 And they were strange to me, as may betide
  With vases, to one deep in Phidian lore.

### II

How is it, Shadows! that I knew ye not?
 How came ye muffled in so hush a mask?
Was it a silent deep-disguised plot
 To steal away, and leave without a task
My idle days? Ripe was the drowsy hour;
 The blissful cloud of summer-indolence
  Benumb'd my eyes; my pulse grew less and less;
Pain had no sting, and pleasure's wreath no flower:
 O, why did ye not melt, and leave my sense
  Unhaunted quite of all but – nothingness?

First printed in 1848.

### III

A third time came they by; – alas! wherefore?
   My sleep had been embroider'd with dim dreams;
My soul had been a lawn besprinkled o'er
   With flowers, and stirring shades, and baffled
                                          beams.
The morn was clouded, but no shower fell,
   Tho' in her lids hung the sweet tears of May;
      The open casement press'd a new-leav'd vine,
   Let in the budding warmth and throstle's lay;
O Shadows! 'twas a time to bid farewell!
      Upon your skirts had fallen no tears of mine.


### IV

A third time pass'd they by, and, passing, turn'd
   Each one the face a moment whiles to me;
Then faded, and to follow them I burn'd
   And ach'd for wings because I knew the three;
The first was a fair Maid, and Love her name;
   The second was Ambition, pale of cheek,
      And ever watchful with fatigued eye;
The last, whom I love more, the more of blame
   Is heap'd upon her, maiden most unmeek, –
      I knew to be my demon Poesy.

## V

They faded, and, forsooth! I wanted wings:
  O folly! What is love! and where is it?
And for that poor Ambition! it springs
  From a man's little heart's short fever-fit;
For Poesy! – no, – she has not a joy, –
  At least for me, – so sweet as drowsy noons,
    And evenings steep'd in honied indolence;
O, for an age so shelter'd from annoy,
  That I may never know how change the moons,
    Or hear the voice of busy common-sense!


## VI

So, ye Three Ghosts, adieu! Ye cannot raise
  My head cool-bedded in the flowery grass;
For I would not be dieted with praise,
  A pet-lamb in a sentimental farce!
Fade softly from my eyes, and be once more
  In masque-like figures on the dreamy urn;
    Farewell! I yet have visions for the night,
And for the day faint visions there is store;
    Vanish, ye Phantoms! from my idle spright,
  Into the clouds, and never more return!

## Ode to Psyche

O Goddess! hear these tuneless numbers, wrung
  By sweet enforcement and remembrance dear,
And pardon that thy secrets should be sung
  Even into thine own soft-conched ear:
Surely I dreamt to-day, or did I see
  The winged Psyche with awaken'd eyes?
I wander'd in a forest thoughtlessly,
  And, on the sudden, fainting with surprise,
Saw two fair creatures, couched side by side
  In deepest grass, beneath the whisp'ring roof
  Of leaves and trembled blossoms, where there ran
    A brooklet, scarce espied:

'Mid hush'd, cool-rooted flowers, fragrant-eyed,
  Blue, silver-white, and budded Tyrian,
They lay calm-breathing on the bedded grass;
  Their arms embraced, and their pinions too;
  Their lips touch'd not, but had not bade adieu,
As if disjoined by soft-handed slumber,
And ready still past kisses to outnumber
  At tender eye-dawn of aurorean love:
    The winged boy I knew;
  But who wast thou, O happy, happy dove?
    His Psyche true!

O latest born and loveliest vision far
  Of all Olympus' faded hierarchy!
Fairer than Phœbe's sapphire-region'd star,
  Or Vesper, amorous glow-worm of the sky;

Fairer than these, though temple thou hast none,
          Nor altar heap'd with flowers;
Nor virgin-choir to make delicious moan
          Upon the midnight hours;
No voice, no lute, no pipe, no incense sweet
     From chain-swung censer teeming;
No shrine, no grove, no oracle, no heat
     Of pale-mouth'd prophet dreaming.

O brightest! though too late for antique vows,
     Too, too late for the fond believing lyre,
When holy were the haunted forest boughs,
     Holy the air, the water, and the fire;
Yet even in these days so far retir'd
     From happy pieties, thy lucent fans,
     Fluttering among the faint Olympians,
I see, and sing, by my own eyes inspir'd.
So let me be thy choir, and make a moan
          Upon the midnight hours;
Thy voice, thy lute, thy pipe, thy incense sweet
     From swinged censer teeming;
Thy shrine, thy grove, thy oracle, thy heat
     Of pale-mouth'd prophet dreaming.

Yes, I will be thy priest, and build a fane
     In some untrodden region of my mind,
Where branched thoughts, new grown with pleasant pain,
     Instead of pines shall murmur in the wind:
Far, far around shall those dark-cluster'd trees
     Fledge the wild-ridged mountains steep by steep;
And there by zephyrs, streams, and birds, and bees,
     The moss-lain Dryads shall be lull'd to sleep;

And in the midst of this wide quietness
A rosy sanctuary will I dress
With the wreath'd trellis of a working brain,
    With buds, and bells, and stars without a name,
With all the gardener Fancy e'er could feign,
    Who breeding flowers, will never breed the same:
And there shall be for thee all soft delight
    That shadowy thought can win,
A bright torch, and a casement ope at night,
    To let the warm Love in!

## Ode on a Grecian Urn

### I

Thou still unravish'd bride of quietness,
　Thou foster-child of silence and slow time,
Sylvan historian, who canst thus express
　A flowery tale more sweetly than our rhyme:
What leaf-fring'd legend haunts about thy shape
　　Of deities or mortals, or of both,
　　　In Tempe or the dales of Arcady?
　What men or gods are these? What maidens loth?
What mad pursuit? What struggle to escape?
　　　What pipes and timbrels? What wild ecstasy?

### II

Heard melodies are sweet, but those unheard
　Are sweeter; therefore, ye soft pipes, play on;
Not to the sensual ear, but, more endear'd,
　Pipe to the spirit ditties of no tone:
Fair youth, beneath the trees, thou canst not leave
　Thy song, nor ever can those trees be bare;
　　　Bold Lover, never, never canst thou kiss,
Though winning near the goal – yet, do not grieve;
　She cannot fade, though thou hast not thy bliss,
　　　For ever wilt thou love, and she be fair!

### III

Ah, happy, happy boughs! that cannot shed
　Your leaves, nor ever bid the Spring adieu;
And, happy melodist, unwearied,
　For ever piping songs for ever new;

More happy love! more happy, happy love!
　　For ever warm and still to be enjoy'd,
　　　For ever panting, and for ever young;
All breathing human passion far above,
　　That leaves a heart high-sorrowful and cloy'd,
　　　A burning forehead, and a parching tongue.


IV

Who are these coming to the sacrifice?
　　To what green altar, O mysterious priest,
Lead'st thou that heifer lowing at the skies,
　　And all her silken flanks with garlands drest?
What little town by river or sea shore,
　　Or mountain-built with peaceful citadel,
　　　Is emptied of this folk, this pious morn?
And, little town, thy streets for evermore
　　Will silent be; and not a soul to tell
　　　Why thou art desolate, can e'er return.


V

O Attic shape! Fair attitude! with brede
　　Of marble men and maidens overwrought,
With forest branches and the trodden weed;
　　Thou, silent form, dost tease us out of thought
As doth eternity: Cold Pastoral!
　　When old age shall this generation waste,
　　　Thou shalt remain, in midst of other woe
Than ours, a friend to man, to whom thou say'st,
　　'Beauty is truth, truth beauty,' – that is all
　　　Ye know on earth, and all ye need to know.

## Ode to a Nightingale

### I

My heart aches, and a drowsy numbness pains
  My sense, as though of hemlock I had drunk,
Or emptied some dull opiate to the drains
  One minute past, and Lethe-wards had sunk:
'Tis not through envy of thy happy lot,
  But being too happy in thine happiness, –
    That thou, light-winged Dryad of the trees,
      In some melodious plot
Of beechen green, and shadows numberless,
  Singest of summer in full-throated ease.

### II

O, for a draught of vintage! that hath been
  Cool'd a long age in the deep-delved earth,
Tasting of Flora and the country green,
  Dance, and Provençal song, and sunburnt mirth!
O for a beaker full of the warm South,
  Full of the true, the blushful Hippocrene,
    With beaded bubbles winking at the brim,
      And purple-stained mouth;
  That I might drink, and leave the world unseen,
    And with thee fade away into the forest dim:

### III

Fade far away, dissolve, and quite forget
  What thou among the leaves hast never known,
The weariness, the fever, and the fret
  Here, where men sit and hear each other groan;

Where palsy shakes a few, sad, last gray hairs,
  Where youth grows pale, and spectre-thin, and dies;
    Where but to think is to be full of sorrow
      And leaden-eyed despairs,
  Where Beauty cannot keep her lustrous eyes,
    Or new Love pine at them beyond to-morrow.

IV

Away! away! for I will fly to thee,
  Not charioted by Bacchus and his pards,
But on the viewless wings of Poesy,
  Though the dull brain perplexes and retards:
Already with thee! tender is the night,
  And haply the Queen-Moon is on her throne,
    Cluster'd around by all her starry Fays;
      But here there is no light,
  Save what from heaven is with the breezes blown
    Through verdurous glooms and winding mossy
                                    ways.

V

I cannot see what flowers are at my feet,
  Nor what soft incense hangs upon the boughs,
But, in embalmed darkness, guess each sweet
  Wherewith the seasonable month endows
The grass, the thicket, and the fruit-tree wild;
  White hawthorn, and the pastoral eglantine;
    Fast fading violets cover'd up in leaves;
      And mid-May's eldest child,
  The coming musk-rose, full of dewy wine,
    The murmurous haunt of flies on summer eves.

## VI

Darkling I listen; and, for many a time
  I have been half in love with easeful Death,
Call'd him soft names in many a mused rhyme,
  To take into the air my quiet breath;
Now more than ever seems it rich to die,
  To cease upon the midnight with no pain,
    While thou art pouring forth thy soul abroad
      In such an ecstasy!
  Still wouldst thou sing, and I have ears in vain –
    To thy high requiem become a sod.

## VII

Thou wast not born for death, immortal Bird!
  No hungry generations tread thee down;
The voice I hear this passing night was heard
  In ancient days by emperor and clown:
Perhaps the self-same song that found a path
  Through the sad heart of Ruth, when, sick for home,
    She stood in tears amid the alien corn;
      The same that oft-times hath
  Charm'd magic casements, opening on the foam
    Of perilous seas, in faery lands forlorn.

## VIII

Forlorn! the very word is like a bell
  To toll me back from thee to my sole self!
Adieu! the fancy cannot cheat so well
  As she is fam'd to do, deceiving elf.
Adieu! adieu! thy plaintive anthem fades
  Past the near meadows, over the still stream,

Up the hill-side; and now 'tis buried deep
    In the next valley-glades:
Was it a vision, or a waking dream?
    Fled is that music: – Do I wake or sleep?

# Ode on Melancholy

### I

No, no, go not to Lethe, neither twist
  Wolf's-bane, tight-rooted, for its poisonous wine;
Nor suffer thy pale forehead to be kiss'd
  By nightshade, ruby grape of Proserpine;
Make not your rosary of yew-berries,
    Nor let the beetle, nor the death-moth be
      Your mournful Psyche, nor the downy owl
A partner in your sorrow's mysteries;
    For shade to shade will come too drowsily,
      And drown the wakeful anguish of the soul.

### II

But when the melancholy fit shall fall
  Sudden from heaven like a weeping cloud,
That fosters the droop-headed flowers all,
  And hides the green hill in an April shroud;
Then glut thy sorrow on a morning rose,
    Or on the rainbow of the salt sand-wave,
      Or on the wealth of globed peonies;
Or if thy mistress some rich anger shows,
    Emprison her soft hand, and let her rave,
      And feed deep, deep upon her peerless eyes.

### III

She dwells with Beauty – Beauty that must die;
  And Joy, whose hand is ever at his lips
Bidding adieu; and aching Pleasure nigh,
  Turning to Poison while the bee-mouth sips:

Ay, in the very temple of delight
   Veil'd Melancholy has her sovran shrine,
      Though seen of none save him whose strenuous
                                 tongue
   Can burst Joy's grape against his palate fine;
His soul shall taste the sadness of her might,
   And be among her cloudy trophies hung.

## To Autumn

Season of mists and mellow fruitfulness,
  Close bosom-friend of the maturing sun;
Conspiring with him how to load and bless
  With fruit the vines that round the thatch-eves run;
To bend with apples the moss'd cottage-trees,
  And fill all fruit with ripeness to the core;
    To swell the gourd, and plump the hazel shells
  With a sweet kernel; to set budding more,
And still more, later flowers for the bees,
Until they think warm days will never cease,
    For Summer has o'er-brimm'd their clammy cells.

II

Who hath not seen thee oft amid thy store?
  Sometimes whoever seeks abroad may find
Thee sitting careless on a granary floor,
  Thy hair soft-lifted by the winnowing wind;
Or on a half-reap'd furrow sound asleep,
  Drows'd with the fume of poppies, while thy hook
    Spares the next swath and all its twined flowers:
And sometimes like a gleaner thou dost keep
  Steady thy laden head across a brook;
  Or by a cyder-press, with patient look,
    Thou watchest the last oozings hours by hours.

Where are the songs of Spring? Ay, where are they?
   Think not of them, thou hast thy music too, –
While barred clouds bloom the soft-dying day,
   And touch the stubble-plains with rosy hue;
Then in a wailful choir the small gnats mourn
   Among the river sallows, borne aloft
      Or sinking as the light wind lives or dies;
And full-grown lambs loud bleat from hilly bourn;
   Hedge-crickets sing; and now with treble soft
   The red-breast whistles from a garden-croft;
      And gathering swallows twitter in the skies.

# A Song

# From *Endymion*

## Book IV, lines 173–81

To Sorrow,
I bade good-morrow,
And thought to leave her far away behind;
But cheerly, cheerly,
She loves me dearly;
She is so constant to me, and so kind:
I would deceive her
And so leave her,
But ah! she is so constant and so kind.

# Narrative Poems

# The Eve of St Agnes

### I

St Agnes' Eve – Ah, bitter chill it was!
The owl, for all his feathers, was a-cold;
The hare limp'd trembling through the frozen grass,
And silent was the flock in woolly fold:
Numb were the Beadsman's fingers, while he told
His rosary, and while his frosted breath,
Like pious incense from a censer old,
Seem'd taking flight for heaven, without a death,
Past the sweet Virgin's picture, while his prayer he saith.

### II

His prayer he saith, this patient, holy man;
Then takes his lamp, and riseth from his knees,
And back returneth, meagre, barefoot, wan,
Along the chapel aisle by slow degrees:
The sculptur'd dead, on each side, seem to freeze,
Emprison'd in black, purgatorial rails:
Knights, ladies, praying in dumb orat'ries,
He passeth by; and his weak spirit fails
To think how they may ache in icy hoods and mails.

St Agnes' Eve falls on 21 Jan.

### III

Northward he turneth through a little door,
And scarce three steps, ere Music's golden tongue
Flatter'd to tears this aged man and poor;
But no – already had his deathbell rung:
The joys of all his life were said and sung:
His was harsh penance on St Agnes' Eve:
Another way he went, and soon among
Rough ashes sat he for his soul's reprieve,
And all night kept awake, for sinners' sake to grieve.

### IV

That ancient Beadsman heard the prelude soft;
And so it chanc'd, for many a door was wide,
From hurry to and fro. Soon, up aloft,
The silver, snarling trumpets 'gan to chide:
The level chambers, ready with their pride,
Were glowing to receive a thousand guests:
The carved angels, ever eager-eyed,
Star'd, where upon their heads the cornice rests,
With hair blown back, and wings put cross-wise on their
breasts.

### V

At length burst in the argent revelry,
With plume, tiara, and all rich array,
Numerous as shadows haunting faerily
The brain, new stuff'd, in youth, with triumphs gay
Of old romance. These let us wish away,
And turn, sole-thoughted, to one Lady there,
Whose heart had brooded, all that wintry day,
On love, and wing'd St Agnes' saintly care,
As she had heard old dames full many times declare.

## VI

They told her how, upon St Agnes' Eve,
Young virgins might have visions of delight,
And soft adorings from their loves receive
Upon the honey'd middle of the night,
If ceremonies due they did aright;
As, supperless to bed they must retire,
And couch supine their beauties, lilly white;
Nor look behind, nor sideways, but require
Of Heaven with upward eyes for all that they desire.

## VII

Full of this whim was thoughtful Madeline:
The music, yearning like a God in pain,
She scarcely heard: her maiden eyes divine,
Fix'd on the floor, saw many a sweeping train
Pass by – she heeded not at all: in vain
Came many a tiptoe, amorous cavalier,
And back retir'd; not cool'd by high disdain,
But she saw not: her heart was otherwhere:
She sigh'd for Agnes' dreams, the sweetest of the year.

## VIII

She danc'd along with vague, regardless eyes,
Anxious her lips, her breathing quick and short:
The hallow'd hour was near at hand: she sighs
Amid the timbrels, and the throng'd resort
Of whisperers in anger, or in sport;
'Mid looks of love, defiance, hate, and scorn,
Hoodwink'd with faery fancy; all amort,
Save to St Agnes and her lambs unshorn,
And all the bliss to be before to-morrow morn.

## IX

So, purposing each moment to retire,
She linger'd still. Meantime, across the moors,
Had come young Porphyro, with heart on fire
For Madeline. Beside the portal doors,
Buttress'd from moonlight, stands he, and implores
All saints to give him sight of Madeline,
But for one moment in the tedious hours,
That he might gaze and worship all unseen;
Perchance speak, kneel, touch, kiss – in sooth such
                                    things have been.


## X

He ventures in: let no buzz'd whisper tell:
All eyes be muffled, or a hundred swords
Will storm his heart, Love's fev'rous citadel:
For him, those chambers held barbarian hordes,
Hyena foemen, and hot-blooded lords,
Whose very dogs would execrations howl
Against his lineage: not one breast affords
Him any mercy, in that mansion foul,
Save one old beldame, weak in body and in soul.


## XI

Ah, happy chance! the aged creature came,
Shuffling along with ivory-headed wand,
To where he stood, hid from the torch's flame,
Behind a broad hall-pillar, far beyond
The sound of merriment and chorus bland:
He startled her; but soon she knew his face,
And grasp'd his fingers in her palsied hand,
Saying, 'Mercy, Porphyro! hie thee from this place:
'They are all here to-night, the whole blood-thirsty race!

### XII

'Get hence! get hence! there's dwarfish Hildebrand;
'He had a fever late, and in the fit
'He cursed thee and thine, both house and land:
'Then there's that old Lord Maurice, not a whit
'More tame for his gray hairs – Alas me! flit!
'Flit like a ghost away.' – 'Ah, Gossip dear,
'We're safe enough; here in this arm-chair sit,
'And tell me how' – 'Good Saints! not here, not here;
'Follow me, child, or else these stones will be thy bier.'

### XIII

He follow'd through a lowly arched way,
Brushing the cobwebs with his lofty plume,
And as she mutter'd 'Well-a – well-a-day!'
He found him in a little moonlight room,
Pale, lattic'd, chill, and silent as a tomb.
'Now tell me where is Madeline,' said he,
'O tell me, Angela, by the holy loom
'Which none but secret sisterhood may see,
'When they St Agnes' wool are weaving piously.'

### XIV

'St Agnes! Ah! it is St Agnes' Eve –
'Yet men will murder upon holy days:
'Thou must hold water in a witch's sieve,
'And be liege-lord of all the Elves and Fays,
'To venture so: it fills me with amaze
'To see thee, Porphyro! – St Agnes' Eve!
'God's help! my lady fair the conjuror plays
'This very night: good angels her deceive!
'But let me laugh awhile, I've mickle time to grieve.'

## XV

Feebly she laugheth in the languid moon,
While Porphyro upon her face doth look,
Like puzzled urchin on an aged crone
Who keepeth clos'd a wond'rous riddle-book,
As spectacled she sits in chimney nook.
But soon his eyes grew brilliant, when she told
His lady's purpose; and he scarce could brook
Tears, at the thought of those enchantments cold,
And Madeline asleep in lap of legends old.

Sudden a thought came like a full-blown rose,
Flushing his brow, and in his pained heart
Made purple riot: then doth he propose
A stratagem, that makes the beldame start:
'A cruel man and impious thou art:
'Sweet lady, let her pray, and sleep, and dream
'Alone with her good angels, far apart
'From wicked men like thee. Go, go! – I deem
'Thou canst not surely be the same that thou didst seem.'

'I will not harm her, by all saints I swear,'
Quoth Porphyro: 'O may I ne'er find grace
'When my weak voice shall whisper its last prayer,
'If one of her soft ringlets I displace,
'Or look with ruffian passion in her face:
'Good Angela, believe me by these tears;
'Or I will, even in a moment's space,
'Awake, with horrid shout, my foemen's ears,
'And beard them, though they be more fang'd than
                                        wolves and bears.'

'Ah! why wilt thou affright a feeble soul?
'A poor, weak, palsy-stricken, churchyard thing,
'Whose passing-bell may ere the midnight toll;
'Whose prayers for thee, each morn and evening,
'Were never miss'd.' – Thus plaining, doth she bring
A gentler speech from burning Porphyro;
So woful, and of such deep sorrowing,
That Angela gives promise she will do
Whatever he shall wish, betide her weal or woe.

## XIX

Which was, to lead him, in close secrecy,
Even to Madeline's chamber, and there hide
Him in a closet, of such privacy
That he might see her beauty unespied,
And win perhaps that night a peerless bride,
While legion'd faeries pac'd the coverlet,
And pale enchantment held her sleepy-eyed.
Never on such a night have lovers met,
Since Merlin paid his Demon all the monstrous debt.

'It shall be as thou wishest,' said the Dame:
'All cates and dainties shall be stored there
'Quickly on this feast-night: by the tambour frame
'Her own lute thou wilt see: no time to spare,
'For I am slow and feeble, and scarce dare
'On such a catering trust my dizzy head.
'Wait here, my child, with patience; kneel in prayer
'The while: Ah! thou must needs the lady wed,
'Or may I never leave my grave among the dead.'

### XXI

So saying, she hobbled off with busy fear.
The lover's endless minutes slowly pass'd;
The dame return'd, and whisper'd in his ear
To follow her; with aged eyes aghast
From fright of dim espial. Safe at last,
Through many a dusky gallery, they gain
The maiden's chamber, silken, hush'd, and chaste;
Where Porphyro took covert, pleas'd amain.
His poor guide hurried back with agues in her brain.

### XXII

Her falt'ring hand upon the balustrade,
Old Angela was feeling for the stair,
When Madeline, St Agnes' charmed maid,
Rose, like a mission'd spirit, unaware:
With silver taper's light, and pious care,
She turn'd, and down the aged gossip led
To a safe level matting. Now prepare,
Young Porphyro, for gazing on that bed;
She comes, she comes again, like ring-dove fray'd and
fled.

### XXIII

Out went the taper as she hurried in;
Its little smoke, in pallid moonshine, died:
She clos'd the door, she panted, all akin
To spirits of the air, and visions wide:
No uttered syllable, or, woe betide!
But to her heart, her heart was voluble,
Paining with eloquence her balmy side;
As though a tongueless nightingale should swell
Her throat in vain, and die, heart-stifled, in her dell.

### XXIV

A casement high and triple-arch'd there was,
    All garlanded with carven imag'ries
Of fruits, and flowers, and bunches of knot-grass,
    And diamonded with panes of quaint device,
    Innumerable of stains and splendid dyes,
As are the tiger-moth's deep-damask'd wings;
    And in the midst, 'mong thousand heraldries,
    And twilight saints, and dim emblazonings,
A shielded scutcheon blush'd with blood of queens and
                                                            kings.

### XXV

Full on this casement shone the wintry moon,
    And threw warm gules on Madeline's fair breast,
As down she knelt for heaven's grace and boon;
    Rose-bloom fell on her hands, together prest,
    And on her silver cross soft amethyst,
And on her hair a glory, like a saint:
    She seem'd a splendid angel, newly drest,
    Save wings, for heaven: – Porphyro grew faint:
She knelt, so pure a thing, so free from mortal taint.

### XXVI

Anon his heart revives: her vespers done,
    Of all its wreathed pearls her hair she frees;
Unclasps her warmed jewels one by one;
    Loosens her fragrant boddice; by degrees
    Her rich attire creeps rustling to her knees:
Half-hidden, like a mermaid in sea-weed,
    Pensive awhile she dreams awake, and sees,
    In fancy, fair St Agnes in her bed,
But dares not look behind, or all the charm is fled.

### XXVII

Soon, trembling in her soft and chilly nest,
In sort of wakeful swoon, perplex'd she lay,
Until the poppied warmth of sleep oppress'd
Her soothed limbs, and soul fatigued away;
Flown, like a thought, until the morrow-day;
Blissfully haven'd both from joy and pain;
Clasp'd like a missal where swart Paynims pray;
Blinded alike from sunshine and from rain,
As though a rose should shut, and be a bud again.

### XXVIII

Stol'n to this paradise, and so entranced,
Porphyro gazed upon her empty dress,
And listen'd to her breathing, if it chanced
To wake into a slumberous tenderness;
Which when he heard, that minute did he bless,
And breath'd himself: then from the closet crept,
Noiseless as fear in a wide wilderness,
And over the hush'd carpet, silent, stept,
And 'tween the curtains peep'd, where, lo! – how fast
she slept.

### XXIX

Then by the bed-side, where the faded moon
Made a dim, silver twilight, soft he set
A table, and, half anguish'd, threw thereon
A cloth of woven crimson, gold, and jet: –
O for some drowsy Morphean amulet!
The boisterous, midnight, festive clarion,
The kettle-drum, and far-heard clarinet,
Affray his ears, though but in dying tone: –
The hall door shuts again, and all the noise is gone.

## XXX

And still she slept an azure-lidded sleep,
In blanched linen, smooth, and lavender'd,
While he from forth the closet brought a heap
Of candied apple, quince, and plum, and gourd;
With jellies soother than the creamy curd,
And lucent syrops, tinct with cinnamon;
Manna and dates, in argosy transferr'd
From Fez; and spiced dainties, every one,
From silken Samarcand to cedar'd Lebanon.

These delicates he heap'd with glowing hand
On golden dishes and in baskets bright
Of wreathed silver: sumptuous they stand
In the retired quiet of the night,
Filling the chilly room with perfume light. –
'And now, my love, my seraph fair, awake!
'Thou art my heaven, and I thine eremite:
'Open thine eyes, for meek St Agnes' sake,
'Or I shall drowse beside thee, so my soul doth ache.'

Thus whispering, his warm, unnerved arm
Sank in her pillow. Shaded was her dream
By the dusk curtains: – 'twas a midnight charm
Impossible to melt as iced stream:
The lustrous salvers in the moonlight gleam;
Broad golden fringe upon the carpet lies:
It seem'd he never, never could redeem
From such a stedfast spell his lady's eyes;
So mus'd awhile, entoil'd in woofed phantasies.

Awakening up, he took her hollow lute, –
Tumultuous, – and, in chords that tenderest be,
He play'd an ancient ditty, long since mute,
In Provence call'd, 'La belle dame sans mercy:'
Close to her ear touching the melody; –
Wherewith disturb'd, she utter'd a soft moan:
He ceased – she panted quick – and suddenly
Her blue affrayed eyes wide open shone:
Upon his knees he sank, pale as smooth-sculptured stone.

## XXXIV

Her eyes were open, but she still beheld,
Now wide awake, the vision of her sleep:
There was a painful change, that nigh expell'd
The blisses of her dream so pure and deep
At which fair Madeline began to weep,
And moan forth witless words with many a sigh;
While still her gaze on Porphyro would keep;
Who knelt, with joined hands and piteous eye,
Fearing to move or speak, she look'd so dreamingly.

## XXXV

'Ah, Porphyro!' said she, 'but even now
'Thy voice was at sweet tremble in mine ear,
'Made tuneable with every sweetest vow;
'And those sad eyes were spiritual and clear:
'How chang'd thou art! how pallid, chill, and drear!
'Give me that voice again, my Porphyro,
'Those looks immortal, those complainings dear!
'Oh leave me not in this eternal woe,
'For if thou diest, my Love, I know not where to go.'

## XXXVI

Beyond a mortal man impassion'd far
At these voluptuous accents, he arose,
Ethereal, flush'd, and like a throbbing star
Seen mid the sapphire heaven's deep repose;
Into her dream he melted, as the rose
Blendeth its odour with the violet, –
Solution sweet: meantime the frost-wind blows
Like Love's alarum pattering the sharp sleet
Against the window-panes; St Agnes' moon hath set.

## XXXVII

'Tis dark: quick pattereth the flaw-blown sleet:
'This is no dream, my bride, my Madeline!'
'Tis dark: the iced gusts still rave and beat:
'No dream, alas! alas! and woe is mine!
'Porphyro will leave me here to fade and pine. –
'Cruel! what traitor could thee hither bring?
'I curse not, for my heart is lost in thine,
'Though thou forsakest a deceived thing; –
'A dove forlorn and lost with sick unpruned wing.'

## XXXVIII

'My Madeline! sweet dreamer! lovely bride!
'Say, may I be for aye thy vassal blest?
'Thy beauty's shield, heart-shap'd and vermeil dyed?
'Ah, silver shrine, here will I take my rest
'After so many hours of toil and quest,
'A famish'd pilgrim, – sav'd by miracle.
'Though I have found, I will not rob thy nest
'Saving of thy sweet self; if thou think'st well
'To trust, fair Madeline, to no rude infidel.

## XXXIX

'Hark! 'tis an elfin-storm from faery land,
'Of haggard seeming, but a boon indeed:
'Arise – arise! the morning is at hand; –
'The bloated wassaillers will never heed: –
'Let us away, my love, with happy speed;
'There are no ears to hear, or eyes to see, –
'Drown'd all in Rhenish and the sleepy mead:
'Awake! arise! my love, and fearless be,
'For o'er the southern moors I have a home for thee.'

She hurried at his words, beset with fears,
For there were sleeping dragons all around,
At glaring watch, perhaps, with ready spears –
Down the wide stairs a darkling way they found. –
In all the house was heard no human sound.
A chain-droop'd lamp was flickering by each door;
The arras, rich with horseman, hawk, and hound,
Flutter'd in the besieging wind's uproar;
And the long carpets rose along the gusty floor.

They glide, like phantoms, into the wide hall;
Like phantoms, to the iron porch, they glide;
Where lay the Porter, in uneasy sprawl,
With a huge empty flaggon by his side:
The wakeful bloodhound rose, and shook his hide,
But his sagacious eye an inmate owns:
By one, and one, the bolts full easy slide: –
The chains lie silent on the footworn stones; –
The key turns, and the door upon its hinges groans.

And they are gone: aye, ages long ago
These lovers fled away into the storm.
That night the Baron dreamt of many a woe,
And all his warrior-guests, with shade and form
Of witch, and demon, and large coffin-worm,
Were long be-nightmar'd. Angela the old
Died palsy-twitch'd, with meagre face deform;
The Beadsman, after thousand aves told,
For aye unsought for slept among his ashes cold.

# From *Lamia*

## Book I, lines 47–62

*(Lamia is first seen as a snake.)*

She was a gordian shape of dazzling hue,
Vermilion-spotted, golden, green, and blue;
Striped like a zebra, freckled like a pard,
Eyed like a peacock, and all crimson barr'd;
And full of silver moons, that, as she breathed,
Dissolv'd, or brighter shone, or interwreathed
Their lustres with the gloomier tapestries –
So rainbow-sided, touch'd with miseries,
She seem'd, at once, some penanced lady elf,
Some demon's mistress, or the demon's self.
Upon her crest she wore a wannish fire
Sprinkled with stars, like Ariadne's tiar:
Her head was serpent, but ah, bitter-sweet!
She had a woman's mouth with all its pearls complete:
And for her eyes: what could such eyes do there
But weep, and weep, that they were born so fair?

## Book I, lines 146–66

*(She begins to change herself into a woman.)*

Left to herself, the serpent now began
To change; her elfin blood in madness ran,
Her mouth foam'd, and the grass, therewith besprent,
Wither'd at dew so sweet and virulent;

Her eyes in torture fix'd, and anguish drear,
Hot, glaz'd, and wide, with lid-lashes all sear,
Flash'd phosphor and sharp sparks, without one cooling
                                                                    tear.

The colours all inflam'd throughout her train,
She writh'd about, convuls'd with scarlet pain:
A deep volcanian yellow took the place
Of all her milder-mooned body's grace;
And, as the lava ravishes the mead,
Spoilt all her silver mail, and golden brede;
Made gloom of all her frecklings, streaks and bars,
Eclips'd her crescents, and lick'd up her stars:
So that, in moments few, she was undrest
Of all her sapphires, greens, and amethyst,
And rubious-argent: of all these bereft,
Nothing but pain and ugliness were left.
Still shone her crown; that vanish'd, also she
Melted and disappear'd as suddenly . . .

## Book II, lines 191–311

*(Lamia's wedding feast, to which her bridegroom Lycius's
old teacher, the philosopher Apollonius, invites himself.)*

When in an antichamber every guest
Had felt the cold full sponge to pleasure press'd,
By minist'ring slaves, upon his hands and feet,
And fragrant oils with ceremony meet
Pour'd on his hair, they all mov'd to the feast
In white robes, and themselves in order placed
Around the silken couches, wondering
Whence all this mighty cost and blaze of wealth could
                                                                    spring.

Soft went the music the soft air along,
While fluent Greek a vowel'd undersong
Kept up among the guests, discoursing low
At first, for scarcely was the wine at flow;
But when the happy vintage touch'd their brains,
Louder they talk, and louder come the strains
Of powerful instruments: – the gorgeous dyes,
The space, the splendour of the draperies,
The roof of awful richness, nectarous cheer,
Beautiful slaves, and Lamia's self, appear,
Now, when the wine has done its rosy deed,
And every soul from human trammels freed,
No more so strange; for merry wine, sweet wine,
Will make Elysian shades not too fair, too divine.
Soon was God Bacchus at meridian height;
Flush'd were their cheeks, and bright eyes double bright:
Garlands of every green, and every scent
From vales deflower'd, or forest-trees branch-rent,
In baskets of bright osier'd gold were brought
High as the handles heap'd, to suit the thought
Of every guest; that each, as he did please,
Might fancy-fit his brows, silk-pillow'd at his ease.

What wreath for Lamia? What for Lycius?
What for the sage, old Apollonius?
Upon her aching forehead be there hung
The leaves of willow and of adder's tongue;
And for the youth, quick, let us strip for him
The thyrsus, that his watching eyes may swim
Into forgetfulness; and, for the sage,
Let spear-grass and the spiteful thistle wage
War on his temples. Do not all charms fly
At the mere touch of cold philosophy?

There was an awful rainbow once in heaven:
We know her woof, her texture; she is given
In the dull catalogue of common things.
Philosophy will clip an Angel's wings,
Conquer all mysteries by rule and line,
Empty the haunted air, and gnomed mine –
Unweave a rainbow, as it erewhile made
The tender-person'd Lamia melt into a shade.

By her glad Lycius sitting, in chief place,
Scarce saw in all the room another face,
Till, checking his love trance, a cup he took
Full brimm'd, and opposite sent forth a look
'Cross the broad table, to beseech a glance
From his old teacher's wrinkled countenance,
And pledge him. The bald-head philosopher
Had fix'd his eye, without a twinkle or stir
Full on the alarmed beauty of the bride,
Brow-beating her fair form, and troubling her sweet
                                                    pride.
Lycius then press'd her hand, with devout touch,
As pale it lay upon the rosy couch:
'Twas icy, and the cold ran through his veins;
Then sudden it grew hot, and all the pains
Of an unnatural heat shot to his heart.
'Lamia, what means this? Wherefore dost thou start?
'Know'st thou that man?' Poor Lamia answer'd not.
He gaz'd into her eyes, and not a jot
Own'd they the lovelorn piteous appeal:
More, more he gaz'd: his human senses reel:
Some hungry spell that loveliness absorbs;
There was no recognition in those orbs.
'Lamia!' he cried – and no soft-toned reply.
The many heard, and the loud revelry

Grew hush; the stately music no more breathes;
The myrtle sicken'd in a thousand wreaths.
By faint degrees, voice, lute, and pleasure ceased;
A deadly silence step by step increased,
Until it seem'd a horrid presence there,
And not a man but felt the terror in his hair.
'Lamia!' he shriek'd; and nothing but the shriek
With its sad echo did the silence break.
'Begone, foul dream!' he cried, gazing again
In the bride's face, where now no azure vein
Wander'd on fair-spaced temples; no soft bloom
Misted the cheek; no passion to illume
The deep-recessed vision: – all was blight;
Lamia, no longer fair, there sat a deadly white.
'Shut, shut those juggling eyes, thou ruthless man!
'Turn them aside, wretch! or the righteous ban
'Of all the Gods, whose dreadful images
'Here represent their shadowy presences,
'May pierce them on the sudden with the thorn
'Of painful blindness; leaving thee forlorn,
'In trembling dotage to the feeblest fright
'Of conscience, for their long offended might,
'For all thine impious proud-heart sophistries,
'Unlawful magic, and enticing lies.
'Corinthians! look upon that grey-beard wretch!
'Mark how, possess'd, his lashless eyelids stretch
'Around his demon eyes! Corinthians, see!
'My sweet bride withers at their potency.'
'Fool!' said the sophist, in an under-tone
Gruff with contempt; which a death-nighing moan
From Lycius answer'd, as heart-struck and lost,
He sank supine beside the aching ghost.
'Fool! Fool!' repeated he, while his eyes still
Relented not, nor mov'd; 'from every ill

'Of life have I preserv'd thee to this day,
'And shall I see thee made a serpent's prey?'
Then Lamia breath'd death breath; the sophist's eye,
Like a sharp spear, went through her utterly,
Keen, cruel, perceant, stinging: she, as well
As her weak hand could any meaning tell,
Motion'd him to be silent; vainly so,
He look'd and look'd again a level – No!
'A serpent!' echoed he; no sooner said,
Than with a frightful scream she vanished:
And Lycius' arms were empty of delight,
As were his limbs of life, from that same night.
On the high couch he lay! – his friends came round –
Supported him – no pulse, or breath they found,
And, in its marriage robe, the heavy body wound.

# From *Hyperion*

## Book I, lines 1–21

*(The old gods are being driven out by the new.)*

Deep in the shady sadness of a vale
Far sunken from the healthy breath of morn,
Far from the fiery noon, and eve's one star,
Sat gray-hair'd Saturn, quiet as a stone,
Still as the silence round about his lair;
Forest on forest hung about his head
Like cloud on cloud. No stir of air was there,
Not so much life as on a summer's day
Robs not one light seed from the feather'd grass,
But where the dead leaf fell, there did it rest.
A stream went voiceless by, still deadened more
By reason of his fallen divinity
Spreading a shade: the Naiad 'mid her reeds
Press'd her cold finger closer to her lips.

    Along the margin-sand large foot-marks went,
No further than to where his feet had stray'd,
And slept there since. Upon the sodden ground
His old right hand lay nerveless, listless, dead,
Unsceptred; and his realmless eyes were closed;
While his bow'd head seem'd list'ning to the Earth,
His ancient mother, for some comfort yet.

Hyperion arose, and on the stars
Lifted his curved lids, and kept them wide
Until it ceas'd; and still he kept them wide:
And still they were the same bright, patient stars.
Then with a slow incline of his broad breast,
Like to a diver in the pearly seas,
Forward he stoop'd over the airy shore,
And plung'd all noiseless into the deep night.

# The Natural World

# From 'I stood tip-toe upon a little hill'

Here are sweet peas, on tip-toe for a flight:
With wings of gentle flush o'er delicate white,
And taper fingers catching at all things,
To bind them all about with tiny rings.

Linger awhile upon some bending planks
That lean against a streamlet's rushy banks,
And watch intently Nature's gentle doings:
They will be found softer than ring-dove's cooings.
How silent comes the water round that bend;
Not the minutest whisper does it send
To the o'erhanging sallows: blades of grass
Slowly across the chequer'd shadows pass.
Why, you might read two sonnets, ere they reach
To where the hurrying freshnesses aye preach
A natural sermon o'er their pebbly beds;
Where swarms of minnows show their little heads,
Staying their wavy bodies 'gainst the streams,
To taste the luxury of sunny beams
Temper'd with coolness. How they ever wrestle
With their own sweet delight, and ever nestle
Their silver bellies on the pebbly sand.
If you but scantily hold out the hand,
That very instant not one will remain;
But turn your eye, and they are there again.
The ripples seem right glad to reach those cresses,
And cool themselves among the em'rald tresses;

First published in 'Poems', 1817.

The while they cool themselves, they freshness give,
And moisture, that the bowery green may live:
So keeping up an interchange of favours,
Like good men in the truth of their behaviours.
Sometimes goldfinches one by one will drop
From low hung branches; little space they stop;
But sip, and twitter, and their feathers sleek;
Then off at once, as in a wanton freak:
Or perhaps, to show their black, and golden wings,
Pausing upon their yellow flutterings.

# From *Endymion*

## Book I, lines 540–52

'This river does not see the naked sky,
Till it begins to progress silverly
Around the western border of the wood,
Whence, from a certain spot, its winding flood
Seems at the distance like a crescent moon:
And in that nook, the very pride of June,
Had I been used to pass my weary eves;
The rather for the sun unwilling leaves
So dear a picture of his sovereign power,
And I could witness his most kingly hour,
When he doth tighten up the golden reins,
And paces leisurely down amber plains
His snorting four . . .'

# From *Hyperion*

## Book I, lines 72–5

As when, upon a tranced summer-night,
Those green-rob'd senators of mighty woods,
Tall oaks, branch-charmed by the earnest stars,
Dream, and so dream all night without a stir . . .

# From 'To J. H. Reynolds, Esq.'

## Lines 86–106

Dear Reynolds! I have a mysterious tale,
And cannot speak it: the first page I read
Upon a Lampit rock of green sea-weed
Among the breakers; 'twas a quiet eve,
The rocks were silent, the wide sea did weave
An untumultuous fringe of silver foam
Along the flat brown sand; I was at home
And should have been most happy, – but I saw
Too far into the sea, where every maw
The greater on the less feeds evermore. –
But I saw too distinct into the core
Of an eternal fierce destruction,
And so from happiness I far was gone.
Still am I sick of it, and tho', to-day,
I've gather'd young spring-leaves, and flowers gay
Of periwinkle and wild strawberry,
Still do I that most fierce destruction see, –
The Shark at savage prey, – the Hawk at pounce, –
The gentle Robin, like a Pard or Ounce,
Ravening a worm, – Away, ye horrid moods!
Moods of one's mind! You know I hate them well.

## On Mrs Reynolds's Cat

Cat! who hast pass'd thy grand climacteric,
   How many mice and rats hast in thy days
   Destroy'd? – How many tit bits stolen? Gaze
With those bright languid segments green, and prick
Those velvet ears – but pr'ythee do not stick
   Thy latent talons in me – and upraise
   Thy gentle mew – and tell me all thy frays
Of fish and mice, and rats and tender chick.
Nay, look not down, nor lick thy dainty wrists –
   For all the wheezy asthma, – and for all
Thy tail's tip is nick'd off – and though the fists
   Of many a maid have given thee many a maul,
Still is that fur as soft as when the lists
   In youth thou enter'dst on glass-bottled wall.

# Light-hearted and
# Nonsense Poems

## Women, Wine, and Snuff

Give me women, wine, and snuff
Until I cry out 'hold, enough!'
You may do so sans objection
Till the day of resurrection;
For bless my beard they aye shall be
My beloved Trinity.

I am as brisk
As a bottle of Wisk-
Ey and as nimble
As a Milliner's thimble.

## I

Where be ye going, you Devon Maid?
    And what have ye there in the Basket?
Ye tight little fairy just fresh from the dairy,
    Will ye give me some cream if I ask it?

## II

I love your Meads, and I love your flowers,
    And I love your junkets mainly,
But 'hind the door I love kissing more,
    O look not so disdainly.

## III

I love your hills, and I love your dales,
    And I love your flocks a-bleating –
But O, on the heather to lie together,
    With both our hearts a-beating!

## IV

I'll put your Basket all safe in a nook,
    Your shawl I hang up on the willow,
And we will sigh in the daisy's eye
And kiss on a grass green pillow.

# A Song about Myself

There was a naughty Boy,
    A naughty boy was he,
He would not stop at home,
    He could not quiet be –
        He took
        In his Knapsack
        A Book
        Full of vowels
        And a shirt
        With some towels –
        A slight cap
        For night cap –
        A hair brush,
        Comb ditto,
        New Stockings
        For old ones
        Would split O!
        This Knapsack
        Tight at's back
        He rivetted close
And followed his Nose
        To the North,
        To the North,
And follow'd his nose
        To the North.

## II

There was a naughty boy
    And a naughty boy was he,
For nothing would he do
    But scribble poetry –
        He took
        An ink stand
        In his hand
        And a pen
        Big as ten
        In the other.
        And away
        In a Pother
        He ran
        To the mountains
        And fountains
        And ghostes
        And Postes
        And witches
        And ditches
        And wrote
        In his coat
        When the weather
        Was cool,
        Fear of gout,
        And without
        When the weather
        Was warm –
        Och the charm
        When we choose

To follow one's nose
   To the north,
   To the north,
To follow one's nose
   To the north!


### III

There was a naughty boy
   And a naughty boy was he,
He kept little fishes
   In washing tubs three
     In spite
     Of the might
     Of the Maid
     Nor afraid
     Of his Granny-good –
     He often would
     Hurly burly
     Get up early
     And go
     By hook or crook
     To the brook
     And bring home
     Miller's thumb,
     Tittlebat
     Not over fat,
     Minnows small
     As the stall
     Of a glove,
     Not above
     The size
     Of a nice

Little Baby's
Little fingers –
O he made
'Twas his trade
Of Fish a pretty Kettle
A Kettle –
A Kettle
Of Fish a pretty Kettle
A Kettle!

IV

There was a naughty Boy,
    And a naughty Boy was he,
He ran away to Scotland
    The people for to see –
        Then he found
        That the ground
        Was as hard,
        That a yard
        Was as long,
        That a song
        Was as merry,
        That a cherry
        Was as red –
        That lead
        Was as weighty,
        That fourscore
        Was as eighty,
        That a door
        Was as wooden
        As in England –

So he stood in his shoes
    And he wonder'd,
    He wonder'd,
He stood in his
    Shoes and he wonder'd.

Pensive they sit, and roll their languid eyes,
Nibble their toast and cool their tea with sighs;
Or else forget the purpose of the night,
Forget their tea, forget their appetite.
See, with cross'd arms they sit – Ah! hapless crew,
The fire is going out and no one rings
For coals, and therefore no coals Betty brings.
A fly is in the milk-pot. Must he die
Circled by a humane Society?
No, no; there, Mr Werter takes his spoon,
Inverts it, dips the handle, and lo! soon
The little struggler, sav'd from perils dark,
Across the teaboard draws a long wet mark.

    Romeo! Arise! take snuffers by the handle,
There's a large cauliflower in each candle.
A winding sheet – ah, me! I must away
To No. 7, just beyond the Circus gay.
'Alas, my friend, your coat sits very well;
Where may your Tailor live?' 'I may not tell.
O pardon me – I'm absent: now and then.
Where *might* my Tailor live? I say again
I cannot tell, let me no more be teas'd;
He lives in Wapping, *might* live where he pleas'd.'

The House of Mourning written by Mr Scott, –
   A sermon at the Magdalen – a tear
   Dropt on a greasy novel, – want of cheer
After a walk up hill to a friend's cot, –
Tea with a Maiden Lady – a curs'd lot
   Of worthy poems with the Author near, –
   A patron lord – a drunkenness from beer, –
Haydon's great picture, – a cold coffee pot
At midnight when the Muse is ripe for labour, –
   The voice of Mr Coleridge, – a french Bonnet
Before you in the pit, – a pipe and tabour, –
A damn'd inseparable flute and neighbour, –
   All these are vile, – but viler Wordsworth's Sonnet
On Dover: – Dover! – who *could* write upon it?

# Letters

*A few extracts from the letters of Keats – mostly his thoughts on poetry.*

. . . O for a Life of Sensations rather than of Thoughts!

[to Benjamin Bailey, 22 Nov. 1817]

∾

One of the three Books I have with me is Shakespeare's Poems: I neer found so many beauties in the sonnets – they seem to be full of fine things said unintentionally – in the intensity of working out conceits – Is this to be borne? Hark ye!

> When lofty trees I see barren of leaves
> Which erst from heat did canopy the herd
> And Summer's green all girded up in sheaves,
> Borne on the bier with white and bristly beard.

He has left nothing to say about nothing or anything.

[the quotation is from Shakespeare's Sonnet 12,
the letter to J. H. Reynolds, 22 Nov. 1817]

∾

I had not a dispute but a disquisition with Dilke, on various subjects; several things dovetailed in my mind, & at once it struck me, what quality went to form a Man of Achievement especially in Literature & which Shakespeare possessed so enormously – I mean *Negative Capability*, that is when a man is capable of being in uncertainties, Mysteries, doubts, without any irritable reaching after fact & reason . . .

[to his brothers George and Tom, Dec. 1817]

∾

We hate poetry that has a palpable design upon us – and if we do not agree, seems to put its hand in its breeches pocket. Poetry should be great & unobtrusive, a thing which enters into one's soul, and does not startle it or amaze it with itself but with its subject. – How beautiful are the retired flowers! how would they lose their beauty were they to throng into the highway crying out, 'admire me I am a violet! dote upon me I am a primrose!'

[to J. H. Reynolds, 3 Feb. 1818]

∾

In Poetry I have a few Axioms, and you will see how far I am from their Centre. 1st I think Poetry should surprise by a fine excess and not by Singularity – it should strike the Reader as a wording of his own highest thoughts, and appear almost a Remembrance – 2nd Its touches of Beauty should never be half way thereby making the reader breathless instead of content: the rise, the progress, the setting of imagery should like the Sun come natural to him – shine over him and set soberly although in magnificence leaving him in the Luxury of twilight –

but it is easier to think what Poetry should be than to write it – and this leads me to another axiom. That if Poetry comes not as naturally as the Leaves to a tree it had better not come at all.

[to his publisher John Taylor, 27 Feb. 1818]

∾

The Genius of Poetry must work out its own salvation in a man: It cannot be matured by law & precept, but by sensation & watchfulness in itself – That which is creative must create itself ... I was never afraid of failure; for I would sooner fail than not be among the greatest.

[to James Hessey, publishing partner of John Taylor, 8 Oct. 1818. Both men admired Keats greatly, and felt affection for him, which he returned]

∾

I think I shall be among the English Poets after my death.
[the simple affirmation comes after mentioning attacks on his work by some critics, in a letter to his brother George and sister-in-law Georgiana, 14 Oct. 1818]

∾

As to the poetical Character itself, (I mean that sort of which, if I am any thing, I am a Member; that sort distinguished from the wordsworthian or egotistical sublime; which is a thing per se and stands alone) it is not itself – it has no self – it is every thing and nothing – It has no character – it enjoys light and shade; it lives in gusto, be it foul or fair, high or low, rich or poor, mean or elevated – It has as much delight in conceiving an Iago as an

Imogen. What shocks the virtuous philosopher, delights the camelion Poet. It does no harm from its relish of the dark side of things any more than from its taste for the bright one; because they both end in speculation. A Poet is the most unpoetical of any thing in existence; because he has no Identity – he is continually informing – and filling some other Body – The Sun, the Moon, the Sea and Men and Women who are creatures of impulse are poetical and have about them an unchangeable attribute – the poet has none; no identity – he is certainly the most unpoetical of all God's Creatures ... I am ambitious of doing the world some good: if I should be spared that may be the work of maturer years – in the interval I will assay to reach to as high a summit in Poetry as the nerve bestowed upon me will suffer ... I feel assured I should write from the mere yearning and fondness I have for the Beautiful even if my night's labours should be burnt every morning and no eye ever shine upon them. But even now I am perhaps not speaking from myself; but from some character in whose soul I now live. I am sure however that this next sentence is from myself. I feel your anxiety, good opinion and friendliness in the highest degree ...

[to Richard Woodhouse, adviser to his publishers, another good friend, 27 Oct. 1818]

☙

... they are very shallow people who take everything literal A Man's life of any worth is a continual allegory ... Lord Byron cuts a figure – but he is not figurative – Shakespeare led a life of Allegory; his works are comments on it –

> [hastily written, like many of his letters, to George and Georgiana Keats, 19 Feb. 1819]

∾

Last Sunday I took a Walk towards Highgate and in the lane that winds by the side of Lord Mansfield's park I met Mr Green our Demonstrator at Guy's in conversation with Coleridge – I joined them, after enquiring by a look whether it would be agreeable – I walked with him at his alderman-after dinner pace for near two miles I suppose. In those two Miles he broached a thousand things – let me see if I can give you a list – Nightingales, Poetry – on poetical sensation – Metaphysics – Different genera and species of Dreams – Nightmare – a dream accompanied by a sense of touch – single and double touch – A dream related – First and second consciousness – the difference explained between will and Volition – so many metaphysicians from a want of smoking the second consciousness – Monsters – the Kraken – Mermaids – Southey believes in them – Southey's belief too much diluted – A Ghost story – Good morning – I heard his voice as he came towards me – I heard it as he moved away – I had heard it all the interval – if it may be called so. He was civil enough to ask me to call on at Highgate Good Night!

> [to George and Georgiana, 15 Apr. 1819]

∾

One of the great reasons that the English have produced the finest writers in the world is, that the English world has ill-treated them during their lives and foster'd them after their deaths. They have in general been trampled aside into the bye paths of life and seen the festerings of Society ... The middle age of Shakespeare was all clouded over; his days were not more happy than Hamlet's who is perhaps more like Shakespeare himself in his common every day Life than any other of his Characters ... I have been very idle lately, very averse to writing; both from the overpowering idea of our dead poets and from abatement of my love of fame. I hope I am a little more of a Philosopher than I was, consequently a little less of a versifying Pet-lamb. I have put no more in Print or you should have had it. You will judge of my 1819 temper when I tell you that the thing I have most enjoyed this year has been writing an ode to Indolence.

[in fact he had just written 'La Belle Dame sans Merci' and 'Ode to a Nightingale', 'Ode on a Grecian Urn', 'Ode on Melancholy' as well as the ode he mentions here to Sarah Jeffreys, daughter of a family in Devonshire who had been friendly with the Keatses; the letter is dated 8 June 1819]

∾

I am convinced more and more day by day that fine writing is next to fine doing the top thing in the world; the Paradise Lost becomes a greater wonder – The more I know what my diligence may in time probably effect; the more does my heart distend with Pride and Obstinacy – I feel it in my power to become a popular writer ... Those whom I know already and who have grown as it were a part of myself I could not do without: but for the rest of Mankind they are as much a dream to me as Milton's Hierarchies. I think if I had a free and healthy and lasting organisation of heart and Lungs – as strong as an ox's – so as to bear unhurt the shock of extreme thought and sensation without weariness, I could pass my Life very nearly alone though it should last eighty years. But I feel my Body too weak to support me to the height; I am obliged continually to check myself and strive to be nothing. It would be vain for me to endeavour after a more reasonable manner of writing to you: I have nothing to speak of but myself – and what can I say but what I feel? If you should have any reason to regret this state of excitement in me, I will turn the tide of your feelings in the right channel by mentioning that it is the only state for the best sort of Poetry – that is all I care for, all I live for.

[to J. H. Reynolds, one of his most intimate friends,
he wrote this heartbreakingly honest account of himself
from Winchester, 24 Aug. 1819]

∾

My dear Girl, I have been hurried to Town by a Letter from my brother George; it is not of the brightest intelligence. Am I mad or not? I came by the Friday night coach – and have not yet been to Hampstead. Upon my soul it is not my fault, I cannot resolve to mix any pleasure with my days: they go one like another undistinguishable. If I were to see you today it would destroy the half comfortable sullenness I enjoy at present into downright perplexities. I love you too much to venture to Hampstead, I feel it is not paying a visit, but venturing into a fire. Que ferai je? as the french novel writers say in fun, and I in earnest: really what can I do? Knowing well that my life must be passed in fatigue and trouble, I have been endeavouring to wean myself from you: for to myself alone what can be much of a misery? As far as they regard myself I can despise all events: but I cannot cease to love you. This morning I scarcely know what I am doing. I am going to Walthamstow – I shall return to Winchester tomorrow; whence you shall hear from me in a few days – I am a Coward, I cannot bear the pain of being unhappy: tis out of the question: I must admit no thought of it. Yours ever affectionately John Keats

[an example of his liveliness and self-tormenting in this
letter to Fanny Brawne, written from Fleet Street, 13 Sept.
1819; Keats made a brief visit to London from Winchester
to sort out some of his brother's money problems, and
did not go to Hampstead]

∾

How beautiful the season is now – How fine the air. A temperate sharpness about it. Really, without joking, chaste weather – Dian skies – I never lik'd stubble fields so much as now – Aye better than the chilly green of the spring. Somehow a stubble plain looks warm – in the same way that some pictures look warm – this struck me so much in my sunday's walk that I composed upon it. I hope you are better employed than in gaping after weather. I have been at different times so happy as not to know what weather it was – No I will not copy a parcel of verses.

[to J. H. Reynolds from Winchester,
21 Sept. 1819; the poem he does not copy
is of course 'To Autumn']

∾

There is one thought enough to kill me – I have been well, healthy, alert &c, walking with her – and now – the knowledge of contrast, feeling for light and shade, all that information (primitive sense) necessary for a poem are great enemies to the recovery of the stomach. There, you rogue, I put you to the torture, – but you must bring your philosophy to bear – as I do mine, really – or how should I be able to live? . . . If I recover, I will do all in my power to correct the mistakes made during sickness; and if I should not, all my faults will be forgiven . . . Write to George as soon as you receive this, and tell him how I am, as far as you can guess; – and also a note to my sister – who walks about my imagination like a ghost – she is so like Tom. I can scarcely bid you good bye even in a letter. I always made an awkward bow. God bless you!
John Keats

[from his last letter, to Charles Brown, dated Rome, 30 Nov. 1820]